OFF TO THE RACES

Airplanes

Thomas Kingsley Troupe

45TH PARALLEL PRESS

Published in the United States of America by Cherry Lake Publishing Group
Ann Arbor, Michigan
www.cherrylakepublishing.com

Reading Adviser: Beth Walker Gambro, MS, Ed., Reading Consultant, Yorkville, IL

PHOTOS CREDITS:
©www.shutterstock.com, cover ©Soos Jozsef, page 2 © Darren Brode | Dreamstime.com, page 4-5 ©© Bruno Ismael Da Silva Alves|Dreamstime.com, page 6-7 © Mika Skye/Shutterstock, page 7 ©CHEN WS, page 8-9_unknown public domain, page 10©public domain (San Diego Air and Space Museum), page 11 ©BlueBarronPhoto, page 12 ©Artinun Prekmoung, page 13 ©Arnold O. A. Pinto, page 14 ©Brphoto, page 15 ©Grekov's, page 16 ©Vladislav S, page17 ©frank_peters, page 18 ©Aleix Ventayol Farrés, page 19 ©mobil11, page 20 ©Nattanon Tavonthammarit, page 21 ©Artinun Prekmoung, page 22 ©Saeedatun, page 23 ©Crystal Craig, page 24 ©betto Rodrigues, page 25 ©Evren Kalinbacak, page 26 ©MRYsportfoto, page 27 ©mobil11 ©Carolyn Hinton Hutchins, page 28 ©Charles Knowles, page 29 ©Soos Jozsef, 30 ©mobil11, 31 ©Igor Karasi, ©www.dreamstime.com

Produced for Cherry Lake Publishing by bluedooreducation.com

45th Parallel Press is an imprint of Cherry Lake Publishing Group.

Library of Congress Cataloging-in-Publication Data has been filed and is available at catalog.loc.gov.
Printed in the United States of America

ABOUT THE AUTHOR

Thomas Kingsley Troupe is the author of over 300 books for young readers. When he's not writing, he enjoys reading, playing video games, and hunting ghosts as part of the Twin Cities Paranormal Society. Otherwise, he's probably taking a nap or something. TKT lives in Woodbury, MN, with his two sons.

Table of Contents

CHAPTER 1
Introduction 4

CHAPTER 2
Airplane Racing History 8

CHAPTER 3
Airplane Racing Events 14

CHAPTER 4
Airplane Racing Classes 20

CHAPTER 5
Airplane Racing Pilots 26

Did You Know? 30
Find Out More 32
Glossary 32
Index 32

Chapter 1

Introduction

The airplane screams with speed. It enters the course. Forces press the pilot back. Hands grip the stick. The plane whistles through the air. The pilot keeps the wings level. The plane goes faster. It zips through the first gate. The pilot jerks the stick. The wings tilt. The plane flies sideways.

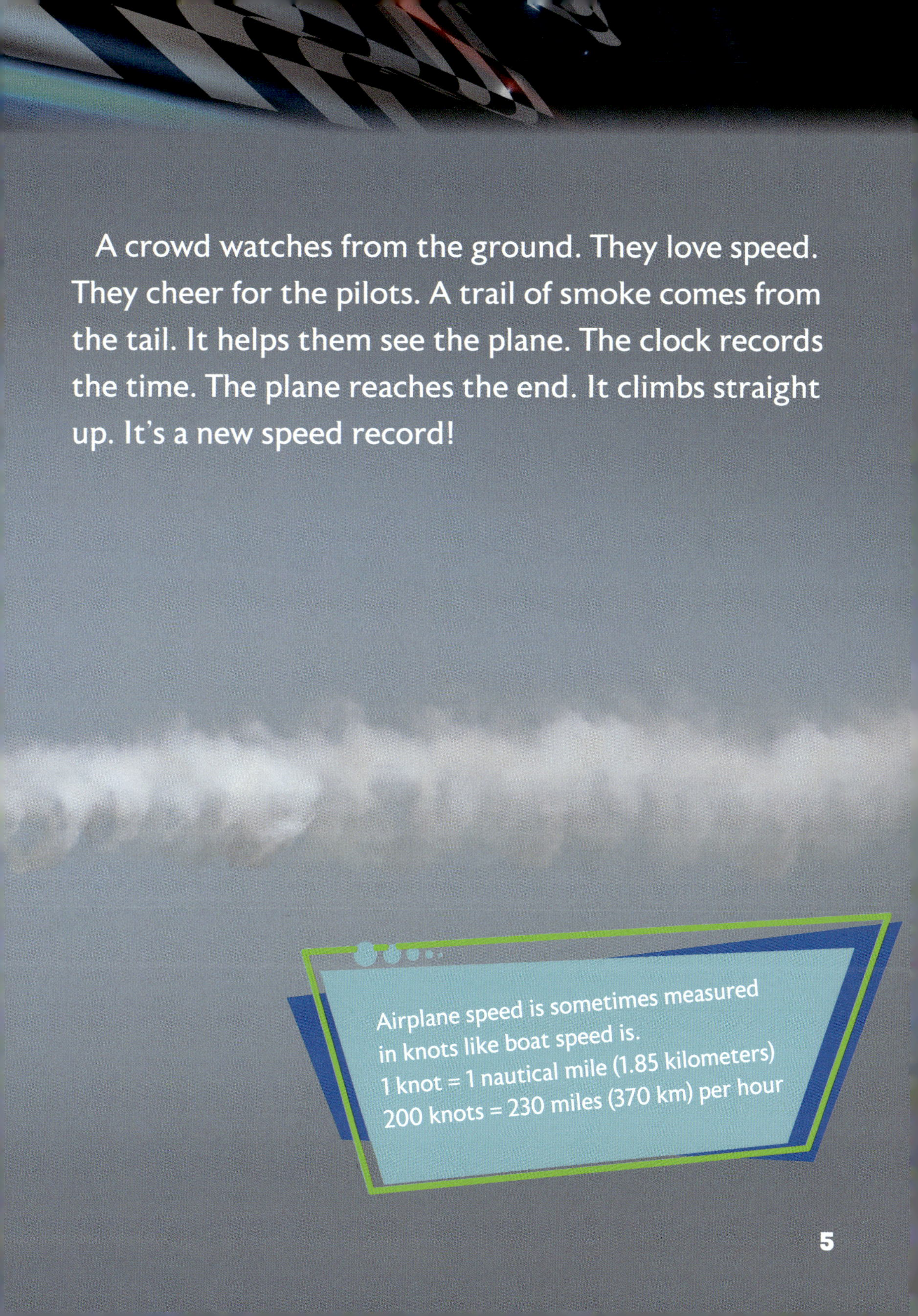

A crowd watches from the ground. They love speed. They cheer for the pilots. A trail of smoke comes from the tail. It helps them see the plane. The clock records the time. The plane reaches the end. It climbs straight up. It's a new speed record!

Airplane speed is sometimes measured in knots like boat speed is.
1 knot = 1 nautical mile (1.85 kilometers)
200 knots = 230 miles (370 km) per hour

Airplane racing is fast and exciting. Pilots crave the feeling of speed. They practice their **maneuvers**. Maneuvers are skillful changes in direction. Pilots will turn, flip, climb, and dive. They sharpen their skills. They know the sport is difficult. Airplane racing is dangerous. They could crash into another plane. The airplane's engine could fail. They risk their lives every time they race. One wrong move could end in tragedy.

Airplane racing is not for the faint of heart. Is the thrill worth the risk? Let's learn more!

Chapter Two

Airplane Racing History

Airplane competitions started in the early 1900s. Airplanes had just been invented. In 1909, people gathered in Reims, France. They were there for Champagne Aviation Week. They wanted to see airplanes in action. There were contests for speed, height, and distance.

Aviation week in Reims, France, 1909

About 500,000 people watched. Some of the planes wouldn't start. A few planes crashed. One dropped out of the sky. Bad weather made it difficult. Crowds still watched. Seeing airplanes fly was a thrill. There were 120 flights at the week-long event.

A crew takes a break under a plane built by the Wright brothers.

The first ever flight happened in 1903. On December 17, Orville Wright flew. It happened in Kitty Hawk, North Carolina. The flight lasted 120 feet (36.57 meters). Orville and his brother Wilbur invented the airplane.

Things changed in 1914. World War I started. Airplane racing paused. Planes were used in battle. The war ended in 1918. Airplane racing came back. Some pilots used war planes. They **modified** them for racing. Modified means changed. Different engines were put in. This made planes faster.

The Sopwith Pup was a fighter plane used in World War I.

Airplane racing grew. World War II began in 1939. The races stopped again. People built new combat planes. The war ended in 1945. Just like before, racers used the designs. The P-51 Mustang plane was popular. It could fly fast and fly far.

The P-51 Mustang was built in the 1940s. It was used as a long-range fighter. It was one of the fastest planes of its time.

Formula 1 air racing started in 1947. Pilots often designed and built their planes. The planes needed to meet **specifications.** Specifications are detailed plans. Planes had to have the same weight. They had to have the same propeller. They had to have the same wingspan too.

In 1970, Formula 1 racing spread. The United Kingdom held events. Soon other countries in Europe did too. The racing craze spread to 4 continents. The event became the Air Race 1 World Cup.

Electric air races are planned for the future. They will be called Air Race E. The planes run on electricity instead of gasoline.

Electric planes are small and lightweight.

Chapter Three

Airplane Racing Events

There are many airplane racing events. The rules change for each class of airplane. A closed course race is one type. It is like a racetrack in the sky. Eight pilots race at the same time. The pilots fly around **pylons**. Pylons are posts or towers that mark the course. The pilots fly laps around the course. They reach incredible speeds. They need the speed to win.

Giant pylons mark the course that the planes must follow.

Closed course races are extremely dangerous. The pilots fly very close to each other. They race at very high speeds. The planes fly at a low altitude. Parachutes can't be opened in time. A crash could be deadly.

Not all air races are held on a course. Long-distance races are about flying far. Pilots all start at one airfield. They must fly to different checkpoints. The checkpoints can be hundreds of miles away. Some distance races are completed in 1 day. Others can take many days. The pilots land. Their time is recorded. The racer with the shortest time wins.

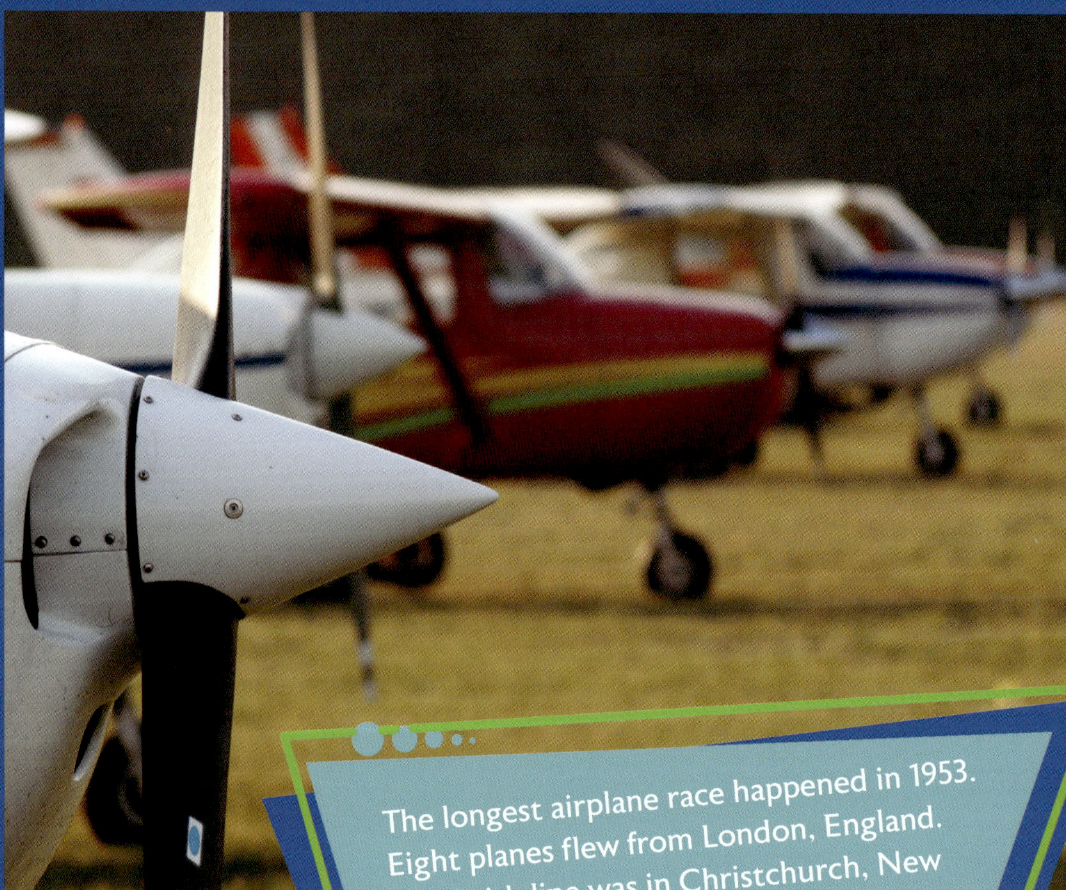

The longest airplane race happened in 1953. Eight planes flew from London, England. The finish line was in Christchurch, New Zealand. The total distance was over 12,000 miles (19,312 km).

The planes are grouped by class. Some classes are based on engine size. Others are sorted by **induction** type. Induction is how the mix of air and fuel is drawn into an engine. There are even experimental plane classes. The different groupings keep the competition fair.

Turboprop biplane

In time trial air racing, pilots race the clock. Time trial air racing is popular. Pilots have to speed through a course. There are pylons set up. They need to fly fast and accurately. The clock starts at the first gate. They make tight turns. The plane turns sideways to weave. At the end, the plane climbs. The planes reach a **g-force** up to 10. G-force is how much the pilot's body feels pushed or pulled when speeding up or slowing down very quickly.

Smoke machines are added to the planes. Smoke leaves a trail behind. It helps the crowd see the plane's run. The entire run is very fast. Some complete the course in under 1 minute. The pilot with the fastest time wins.

Chapter Four

Airplane Racing Classes

There are several airplane racing classes, or categories. Each class has its own unique features and abilities.

Many Formula 1 airplanes are built by their pilots. They design and fly them in races. They have to weigh 500 pounds (227 kilograms) when empty. The wings must be 66 square feet (6.1 square meters). The landing gear is fixed. This means the landing gear is attached to the airplane and stays in the same position. The planes reach speeds of 250 miles (402 km) per hour.

Formula 1 planes are considered cheap. The planes cost between $8,000 to $20,000 to build. It is a great racing class for new pilots. There are several F1 airplane races each year.

Sport Class is another racing class. Planes in Sport Class are kit-built aircraft. This means all the parts come in a set. The plane is assembled following instructions. The engine needs to be **internal combustion**. Internal combustion is the process of burning fuels, such as gasoline, to power an engine. The engine can't be bigger than 1,000 cubic inches (0.016 cubic meters). The planes reach speeds of nearly 350 miles (563 km) per hour.

Sport Class kit-built planes race to the finish.

Experimental designs happen in Sport Class. Builders try new ideas. The ideas help advance high-performance planes. Designers work to get the engines running faster. They make changes to the plane's airframe. They hope the improvements will win races.

The Unlimited Class is popular in airplane racing. The planes are mostly modified World War II fighters. P-51 Mustangs, F-8F Bearcats, and Hawker Sea Furies are used most often. There are only 2 rules for Unlimited Class. The planes must be **piston-powered** and propeller-driven. Piston-powered is a type of internal combustion engine. It is different from a turbojet engine.

The Bearcat was used by the US Navy. It could takeoff and land from an aircraft carrier.

The P-51 Mustang was created in 1944. There were 8,000 of them made.

Airplane racing started with the Unlimited Class. It's also the fastest. The planes reach speeds over 500 miles (804.67 km) per hour! The races are low-flying. They're only 50 to 100 feet (15.24 to 30.48 m) off the ground.

Chapter Five

Airplane Racing Pilots

Airplane racing isn't easy. It takes pilots years of training. They complete thousands of flights. A good pilot has quick reflexes. They have great hand-eye **coordination**. Coordination means parts of the body are working well together. The pilots have to handle high pressure. They need to know how the plane works. Many pilots are mechanics too.

Airplane racing is dangerous. A racing pilot must understand the risks. High speeds and tricky maneuvers can go wrong. They need to be fearless.

Pilots wear a mic and headphones to communicate with the ground crew.

Teamwork is also important. Pilots need to communicate with their crew. They need to listen to the team on the ground.

A flight crew helps the pilot maintain the airplane.

Airplane racing is here to stay. It is a fast and fun sport. It is incredible to think that the sport began just a few years after the first-ever flight. Back then, people wanted to see planes in action. Pilots tried to give them a show. They still do! Today's pilots live for the excitement they feel while racing.

Events and planes continue to change. Races will look different in the future. Planes will get better and faster. They will only get more and more exciting. See if there's an airplane race happening near you. Watch the sport for yourself. Off to the races!

Did You Know?

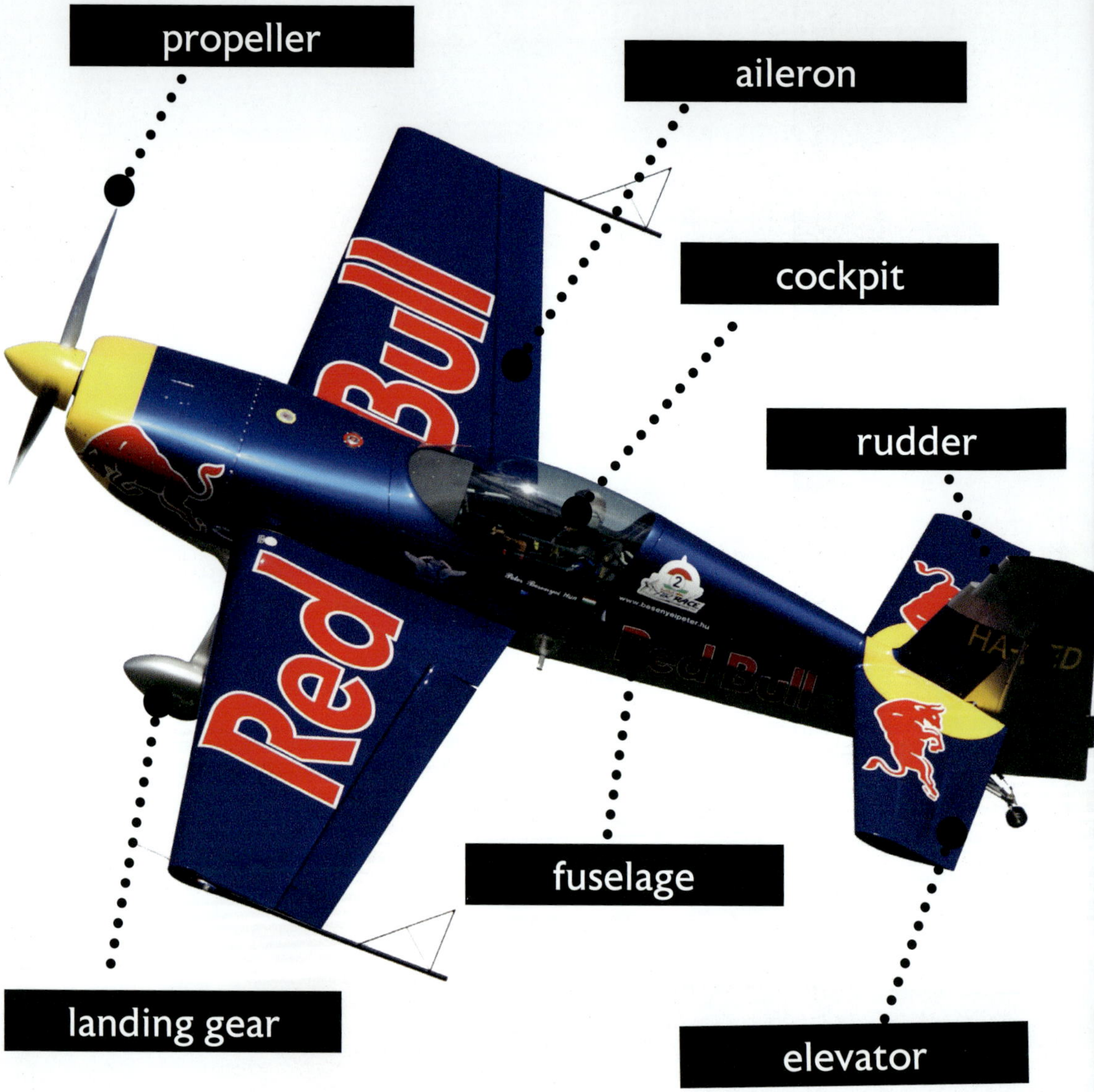
propeller
aileron
cockpit
rudder
fuselage
landing gear
elevator
Red Bull

aileron: controls plane's altitude, or height
cockpit: where the pilot sits
elevator: controls plane's pitch, or angle
fuselage: the main body of the plane
propeller: moves air backwards, which thrusts plane forward
rudder: moves plane side to side

inside cockpit

Find Out More

BOOKS

Farndon, John. *Megafast Planes*. Minneapolis, MN: Lerner Publishing, 2016.

Hamilton, S.L. *The World's Fastest Planes*. Minneapolis, MN: Abdo Publishing, 2021.

WEBSITES

Search these online sources with an adult:

P-51 Mustang | Kiddle

The Wright Brothers | National Geographic Kids

Glossary

coordination (koh-or-duh-NAY-shuhn) ability to use different body parts to complete a task easily

g-force (GEE-fors) a measure of how much a body feels pushed or pulled when accelerating or decelerating really fast

induction (in-DUHK-shuhn) the process of air and fuel being drawn into an engine

internal combustion (ihn-TUR-nuhl kuhm-BUHSH-chuhn) the energy gasoline makes when it burns inside of an engine

maneuvers (muh-NOO-vurz) movements or changes in direction requiring skill

modified (MAH-duh-fyed) changed

piston-powered (PIH-stuhn POW-urd) using pistons, a part of an engine that moves fuel and air into a small space

pylons (PIE-lahnz) posts or towers that mark a race course

specifications (speh-suh-fuh-KAY-shuhnz) a set of requirements or details to be followed

Index

cockpit 30, 31

engine(s) 6, 10, 17, 22, 23, 24

Formula 1 12, 20, 21

Long distance 16

P-51 Mustang 11, 24, 25

speed(s) 4-6, 8, 14, 15, 18, 20, 22, 25, 26

Sport Class 22, 23

time trial 18

Unlimited Class 24, 25

World War I 10

World War II 11, 24